Understanding God

Student Workbook

Joy Hughes Gruits

Acknowledgements:

To my mother-in-law, Patricia Beall Gruits, thank you for the confidence you placed in me to write this Leader's Guide to accompany your inspired book, UNDERSTANDING GOD.

To my sisters, Patricia and Tracie, thank you for setting aside time from your busy schedules to review and edit the manuscript. Your perspective helped bring a greater continuity to this guide for which I am extremely grateful.

To Allison, how wonderful to have a daughter who is such an accomplished teacher who can be such an effective sounding board.

To my niece, Christen, your competence was only matched by your efficient computer skills. Your diligence and willingness to help was a blessing from God.

To Stan Ferguson, your expertise continues to be an invaluable part of the UNDERSTANDING GOD Program.

To Joe, my husband, your unwavering support inspired me to persevere even when the task seemed overwhelming.

Cover Design by Manuel Rivas
Chapter Clipart by Thomas Helland

Scripture marked KJV is taken from the King James Version of the Bible, or marked NIV is taken from The Holy Bible, New International Version (NIV). Copyright © 1973, 1978, 1984 International Bible Society. Used by permission of Zondervan. All rights reserved. Scripture marked NLT is taken from the Holy Bible, New Living Translation, copyright 1996. Used by permission of Tyndale House Publishers, Inc., Wheaton, Illinois 60189. All rights reserved.

UNDERSTANDING GOD Leader Guide

Fore more information contact:

PeterPat Publishers, LLC
P.O. Box 82085
Rochester, Michigan 48308-2085
(248) 608-8050
Fax (248) 608-8055
www.peterpat.com

Library of Congress
ISBN: 0-9639461-7-X

Printed in Canada

This is what I have asked of God for you . . .

that you will have the rich experience of knowing

Christ with real certainty and clear understanding.

Colossians 2:2 (TLB)

INTRODUCTION

The *UNDERSTANDING GOD Student Workbook* was developed to facilitate your understanding of the truths and concepts presented in the book *UNDERSTANDING GOD* by Patricia Beall Gruits. It is a book that will guide you in your study of The Bible as you learn and experience the powerful foundational truths of God's Word.

This workbook is divided into two sections. The first section, Part One, consists of activities that will provoke questions, help you find answers, and solidify your understanding of the lesson material. Theses activities can be completed individually, with a partner or in a small group.

The second section, Part Two, consists of Study Questions. If you are part of an *UNDERSTANDING GOD* class, these questions will be completed during the week after the lesson has been taught. If you are using the book *UNDERSTANDING GOD* for personal study, these questions can be completed after studying each chapter. The purpose of these questions is to stimulate and expand your understanding of the lesson material.

It is my sincere hope this *UNDERSTANDING GOD Student Workbook* will prove to be a valuable aid as you seek a greater understanding of God which will deepen your relationship with Him.

Joy Hughes Gruits

TABLE OF CONTENTS

TABLE OF CONTENTS (cont.)

TABLE OF CONTENTS *(cont.)*

TABLE OF CONTENTS (cont.)

TABLE OF CONTENTS (cont.)

Part Two: Study Questions

TABLE OF CONTENTS (cont.)

TABLE OF CONTENTS (*cont.*)

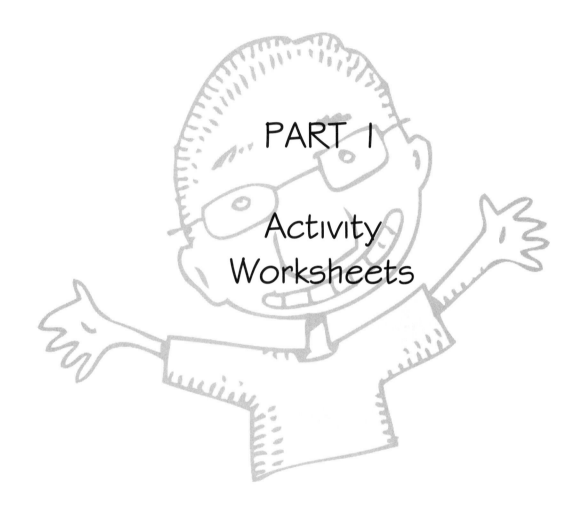

PART 1

Activity Worksheets

CHAPTER 1: UNDERSTANDING GOD

Activity: God Is . . .

Describe a quality God possesses that begins with the letters below. God is . . .

A _____   N _____

B _____   O _____

C _____   P _____

D _____   Q _____

E _____   R _____

F _____   S _____

G _____   T _____

H _____   U _____

I _____   V _____

J _____   W _____

K _____   X _____

L _____   Y _____

M _____   Z _____

CHAPTER 1: UNDERSTANDING GOD

Activity: God Is Even More

Question 1.9 in the *UNDERSTANDING GOD* book lists many attributes of God. However, there are even more to be found in The Bible. Use the Scriptures provided below to discover these attributes.

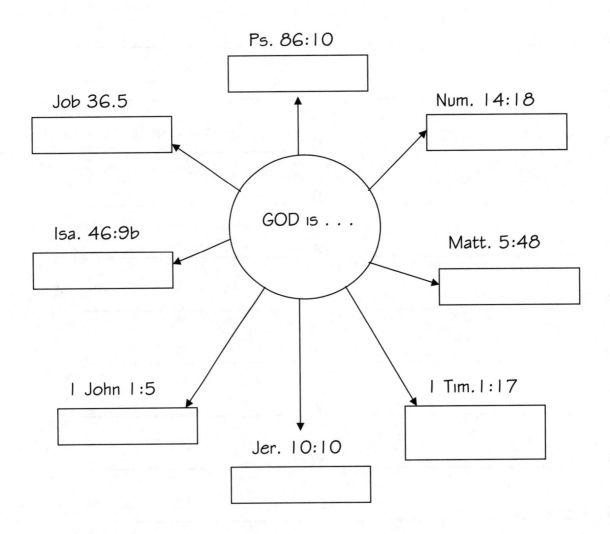

Ps. 86:10

Job 36.5

Num. 14:18

Isa. 46:9b

GOD is . . .

Matt. 5:48

I John 1:5

I Tim. 1:17

Jer. 10:10

CHAPTER 2: UNDERSTANDING THE BIBLE

Activity: Bible Translations

The Bible texts were originally written in the Hebrew, Greek or Aramaic, which means our English Bibles are translations. Read the following verses of The Bible in the four translations listed below. Compare the translations. Note the type of translation (i.e. literal, phrase (thought-for-thought), paraphrase) and the strength of each translation.

Scriptures: Prov. 28:6; Rom. 12:2; 1 Cor. 13:1-5; 2 Cor. 9:8; Eph.1:4-6

	Type of Translation	What is the strength of this translation?
New King James Version (NKJ)		
New Living Translation (NLT)		
New International Version (NIV)		
The Message (MSG)		

What is the advantage of reading various translations of The Bible?

CHAPTER 3: UNDERSTANDING THE SPIRIT WORLD

Activity: The Purpose-Driven Angel

1. Angels were created with a purpose. Using the *UNDERSTANDING GOD* book and The Bible, write down the reasons angels were created in the left column. What is the purpose of their existence?

2. In the right column, brainstorm why you think we were created? What is the purpose of our existence?

Angels	Man

3. How is the purpose of angels and man similar?

CHAPTER 3: UNDERSTANDING THE SPIRIT WORLD

Activity: Fact Or Fiction

Determine whether the following statements about angels are fact or fiction.

FACT   FICTION

_____   _____   1. Angels were created to minister to God and to be ministers of God.

_____   _____   2. Just as humans are occupants of the natural world, angels are occupants of the spirit world.

_____   _____   3. Angels are omnipotent and omnipresent.

_____   _____   4. Angels are equal in rank and position.

_____   _____   5. Angels can reproduce; this is why The Bible speaks of angels being so great in number.

_____   _____   6. It can be dangerous to become angel conscious.

_____   _____   7. Angels are aware of what is going on in our world.

_____   _____   8. Demons are angels who rebelled against God.

_____   _____   9. Lucifer sinned when he coveted God's position as God.

_____   _____   10. Demons have greater powers than angels.

_____   _____   11. Hell was not made for man but for Satan and His demons.

_____   _____   12. Jesus Christ has given Christians power over Satan and his demons.

- 5 -

CHAPTER 4: UNDERSTANDING THE CREATION

Activity: Six Days Of Creation

What did God create on Day 1? Put an "X" in the box for the thing or things God created on Day 1. Now do the same for the rest of the days.

	LAND	MAN	MOON	SKY	LAND ANIMALS	FISH	SUN	DAY (LIGHT)	STARS	FOWL	PLANTS	SEAS	NIGHT
Day 1													
Day 2													
Day 3													
Day 4													
Day 5													
Day 6													

CHAPTER 5: UNDERSTANDING GOD'S COVENANTS WITH MAN

Activity: *God's Covenants*

Fill in the chart below.

What I already knew about God's covenants!	What I have now learned about God's covenants!	What I still want to know about God's covenants! (Questions I still have)

CHAPTER 6: UNDERSTANDING GOD'S COVENANT WITH ADAM

Activity: The Adamic Covenant

1. TERMS of the COVENANT

IF	
THEN	

2. Adam and Eve chose to be _____ of God.

   Adam and Eve _____ covenant with God.
   (kept / broke)

3. RESULTS of their choice:

1.	
2.	
3.	
4.	
5.	

CHAPTER 7: UNDERSTANDING GOD'S COVENANT WITH NOAH

Activity: The Noahic Covenant

1. TERMS of the COVENANT

IF	
THEN	

2. Noah _____ covenant with God.
   (kept / broke)

3. RESULTS of his choice:

1.	
2.	

4. What promise does God make to Noah and his descendants?
   (See Gen. 9:8-17)

5. What is the sign of God's promise to man?

CHAPTERS 6 & 7: UNDERSTANDING GOD'S COVENANTS ADAM - NOAH

Activity: Adam And Noah

GOD'S COVENANT WITH:	IF	THEN	KEPT / BROKE COVENANT	RESULTS OF THEIR CHOICE
ADAM & EVE				
NOAH				

CHAPTER 7: UNDERSTANDING GOD'S COVENANT WITH NOAH

Activity: Fact Or Fiction

Decide if the following statements are fact or fiction.

<u>FACT</u>   <u>FICTION</u>

_____ _____ 1. Only a millennium after the Fall of Adam and Eve, the people on earth have become corrupt and evil. The earth is filled with violence.

_____ _____ 2. Noah was a just and righteous man living in a corrupt world.

_____ _____ 3. God told Noah to build an ark, but Noah had to design it himself.

_____ _____ 4. It is believed it took Noah and his sons about one hundred years to build the ark.

_____ _____ 5. Noah preached while he built the ark, warning people of the coming flood. Many people repented and turned to God.

_____ _____ 6. Before God sent the forty days of rain, it had never rained before.

_____ _____ 7. God not only sent torrential rains but also caused subterranean waters to erupt.

_____ _____ 8. Noah and his family along with pairs of animals were in the ark for about two months.

_____ _____ 9. The first thing Noah did when he left the ark was to kiss the ground.

_____ _____ 10. The rainbow was a sign of God's promise to never again destroy the earth with a flood.

_____ _____ 11. Through Noah and his family, God was giving mankind a fresh start.

_____ _____ 12. Noah allowed God to direct his steps and show him a way of salvation.

CHAPTER 8: UNDERSTANDING GOD'S COVENANT WITH ABRAHAM

Activity: Timeline

Place the events in Abraham and Sarah's life in chronological order. Place the letter of each event in the correct order on the timeline. Use Chapter 8 in the *UNDERSTANDING GOD book* and Genesis 12-22.

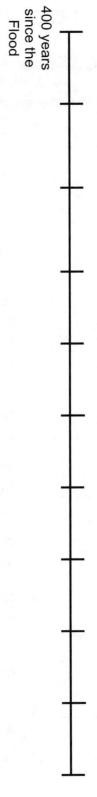

400 years
since the
Flood

A. Abraham prepares to sacrifice Isaac.

B. God meets Abram. God promises Abram great blessings including becoming the father of a great nation.

C. After years of waiting for a miracle, Sarah who is barren suggests that Abraham take Hagar, Sarah's handmaiden, as his second wife. Hagar would be a surrogate mother who would bear a son for them.

D. God reiterates His promise that Abraham and Sarah would have a son. Abraham believes God and because of his faith God "counts" him righteous. God then cuts a blood covenant with Abraham.

E. Abraham and Sarah leave the city of Ur.

F. God leads them to the land of Canaan.

G. Sarah's plan goes awry. Hagar has a son, but she does not give the boy to Sarah. Ishmael is regarded as Abraham and Hagar's son, not Sarah's. Jealousy and hatred fill the house of Abraham.

H. An angel keeps Abraham from sacrificing his son. God blesses Abraham even more because of his great faith in God.

I. Abraham and all the males of his household are physically circumcised as a sign of being in covenant with God.

J. When Sarah is 90 years old and Abraham is 100 years old, God performs a miracle and Isaac, the promised son, is born.

CHAPTER 8: UNDERSTANDING GOD'S COVENANT WITH ABRAHAM

Activity: The Abrahamic Covenant

1. TERMS of the COVENANT

IF	
THEN	

2. Abraham and Sarah _____ covenant with God.
(kept / broke)

3. RESULTS of their choice:

1.	
2.	

4. What was the sign or token of God's covenant with Abraham?

5. What was the most important promise that was fulfilled by God?

CHAPTER 9: UNDERSTANDING GOD'S COVENANT WITH MOSES

Activity: The Mosaic Covenant (Covenant with the Israelites)

1. TERMS of the COVENANT

IF the Israelites	
THEN God	

2. The Israelites _____ covenant with God.
   (kept / broke)

3. RESULTS of their choice:

1.	
2.	

4. What were the laws the nation of Israel were to obey?

   a.

   b.

CHAPTERS 8 & 9:   UNDERSTANDING GOD'S COVENANTS ABRAHAM – MOSES
AND THE ISRAELITES

Activity: Abraham And Moses/Israelites

GOD'S COVENANT WITH:	IF	THEN	KEPT / BROKE COVENANT	RESULTS OF THEIR CHOICE
ABRAHAM				
MOSES/ ISRAELITES				

CHAPTER 10: UNDERSTANDING GOD'S COVENANT WITH DAVID

Activity: How Can That Be?

Both King Saul and King David committed sin, yet the consequences of their sin seem inequitable. When Saul disobeyed God's instructions, God took from him the kingship and the promise of an eternal dynasty. However, when David committed murder and adultery, which seems to be sin of far greater magnitude, God did not take from him the kingship or the promise of an eternal dynasty.

Using the Scriptures given below and the *UNDERSTANDING GOD* book, attempt to answer the question: How can that be?

Saul	David
• 1 Sam. 15:2-26 (TLB)	• 2 Sam. 12:7-10
	• 2 Sam. 7:1-29

1. Why do you think the consequences for Saul were more severe than for David?

2. What lessons can we learn from King Saul and King David?

CHAPTER 10: UNDERSTANDING GOD'S COVENANT WITH DAVID

Activity: Same Yet Different

What covenant promises does God make with David?

Why did God make this covenant with David?

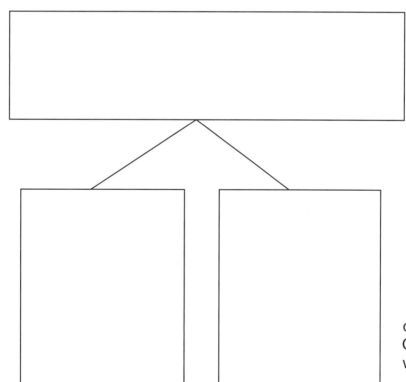

How is this covenant similar to the other covenants God made with man?

How is this covenant different from the other covenants God made with man?

CHAPTER 6-10: UNDERSTANDING GOD'S COVENANTS

Activity: A Review Of The Covenants

For each of the following statements, determine to whom or to which covenant it belongs. There may be statements that apply to more than covenant.

Statements about the Covenants	Adam	Noah	Abraham	Moses	David
1. He and his descendants would become a great nation.					
2. He spent years building an ark as God commanded.					
3. He ate of the Tree of Knowledge of Good and Evil.					
4. He left his country and his relatives as God commanded.					
5. Because of his disobedience, sin entered the human race.					
6. He killed a Philistine giant warrior before becoming king.					
7. He was raised in the house of Pharaoh.					
8. A man of great faith; he believed for the impossible promise of a son.					
9. He built an altar unto God; God promised not to destroy the earth again with a flood.					
10. Because he broke covenant with God, the nature of man was changed.					
11. He committed murder and adultery, causing the iniquity of murder and strife to plague his family.					
12. The first man to witness rain.					

CHAPTER 6-10: UNDERSTANDING GOD'S COVENANTS

Activity: A Review Of The Covenants (Continued)

Statements about the Covenants	Adam	Noah	Abraham	Moses	David
13. God gave him the Ten Commandment, the Levitical Laws, and the blueprint for the Tabernacle of God.					
14. God established a covenant with him promising to make his name great and bless him.					
15. God established a covenant promising safety from certain death.					
16. God established a covenant promising him dominion, power and fruitfulness upon the earth.					
17. God established a covenant promising his kingdom would be eternal.					
18. Jesus Christ was a descendant of this man.				·	
19. God promised him a great natural AND spiritual nation.					
20. God commanded him to be fruitful, multiply, and fill the earth.					
21. God wanted to be his source of wisdom; God wanted to direct the steps of his life.					

CHAPTER II: UNDERSTANDING JESUS CHRIST

Activity: For Unto Us A Child Is Born

Using the *UNDERSTANDING* GOD book and the Scriptures below, place the events of Jesus' life in chronological order.

_____ A. John the Baptist announces the coming of the Messiah.

_____ B. Jesus is born in a stable in Bethlehem.

_____ C. Jesus is taken to Egypt by Joseph and Mary because King Herod wants to kill him.

_____ D. Jesus is buried in a tomb.

_____ E. The angel Gabriel appears to a virgin girl named Mary, announcing she would become pregnant and have a baby boy, the Son of God.

_____ F. Angels announce the birth of Christ to shepherds.

_____ G. Jesus delivers the Sermon on the Mount, teaches with parables, and performs miracles.

_____ H. Jesus is resurrected from the dead, proving His divinity.

_____ I. The wise men worship Jesus and present Him gifts of gold, frankincense, and myrrh.

_____ J. Jesus and his family live in Nazareth.

_____ K. Jesus is crucified on a cross.

_____ M. When Mary and Joseph take Jesus to the temple, Simeon and Anna recognize him as the promised king.

_____ N. King Herod tries to kill infant Jesus.

Source Scriptures:
Luke 1:30-35   Matt. 2:8-23   Matt. 3:11-17   John 19:40-42
Luke 2:4-20   Matt. 3:1-6   John 19:17-19   John 16:1-6

CHAPTER 11: UNDERSTANDING JESUS CHRIST

Activity: Fulfilling Prophecies

Using The Bible, read the Old Testament prophecies and the scriptures in the New Testament that document the life of Jesus Christ. Read the Old Testament scripture to determine what is predicted and then read the New Testament scripture to show how Jesus fulfilled that prophecy.

Old Testament Prophecy	What did the prophecy predict?	New Testament Scripture	How did Jesus fulfill this prophesy?
Isaiah 7:14		Matt. 1:18-23 Luke 1:26-35	
Isaiah 9:1-2		Matt. 4:13-16 Mark 1:14-15	
Isaiah 40:3-5		Matt. 3:3 Mark 1:3	
Isaiah 50:4-6		Matt. 26:67 Mark 14:65 Luke 22:63	
Eze. 34:23-24		John 10:11, 14,16 Heb. 13:20	
Micah 5:2		Matt. 2:1-6	
Zech. 9:9		Matt. 21:1-9 Mark 11:1-10	
Isa. 53:7		Matt. 27:13-14	
Zech. 12:10		John 19:34-37	
Isaiah 53:9		Matt. 27:57-60	

CHAPTER 12: UNDERSTANDING THE INCARNATION OF JESUS CHRIST

Worksheet A

Activity: Adam And Jesus

God the Son had to be incarnated as a human being because of Adam's actions. With a partner compare Adam and Jesus. In what ways are they similar? In what way are they different?

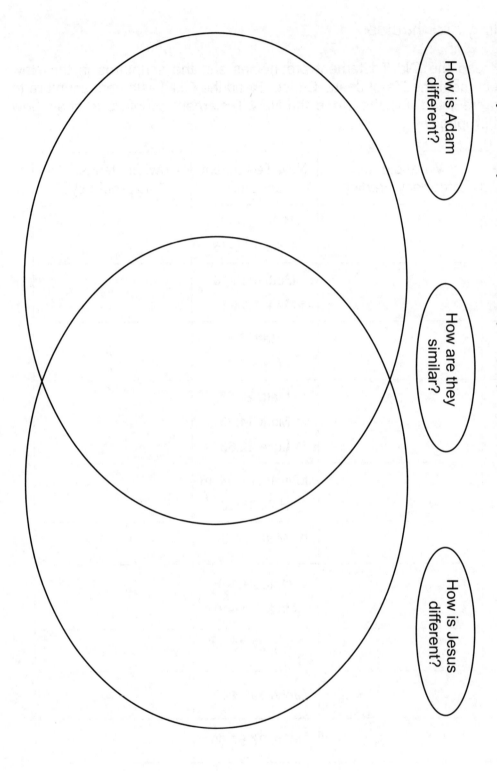

How is Adam different?

How are they similar?

How is Jesus different?

CHAPTER 13: UNDERSTANDING THE NEW COVENANT

Activity: Old Covenant Versus New Covenant

Using the *UNDERSTANDING GOD* book and The Bible, compare the New Covenant with the Old Covenant.

	Old Covenant	New Covenant
What is the duration of this covenant?		
Who can be a part of this covenant?		
Where are God's commandments written?		
What kind of relationship can you have with God in this covenant?		
How is sin dealt with in this covenant?		

Which covenant do you think is the better and more powerful covenant? Explain your answer.

CHAPTER 14: UNDERSTANDING CHRIST'S RESURRECTION AND ASCENSION

Activity: From Death To Resurrection And Ascension

Place in chronological order the events of Jesus' life from His death to His ascension into heaven. Number them 1 through 8.

_____ A. He is on the earth for forty days.

_____ B. He sits at the right hand of God the Father as our Prophet, Priest, and King.

_____ C. He is laid in the tomb.

_____ D. His spirit and soul go to hell (Hades/Sheol).

_____ E. He suffers and dies for us.

_____ F. He releases the righteous dead to go into the presence of God.

_____ G. His body is in the grave three days. His body does not decay.

_____ H. He ascends (rises) to heaven.

CHAPTER 14: UNDERSTANDING CHRIST'S RESURRECTION AND ASCENSION

Activity: The Resurrected Body Of Christ

How is the resurrected body of Christ similar to and different from His human body which was crucified on the Cross?

The Human Body of Christ		The Resurrected Body of Christ
DIFFERENCES	SIMILARITIES	DIFFERENCES

Resource Scriptures: Luke 24:13-43; John 20:14-16; John 20:19-27; Mark 16:12-13

CHAPTER 15: UNDERSTANDING SIN AND INQUITY

Activity: Sin And Iniquity

Below is a list of statements dealing with Actual Sin, Original Sin, and Iniquity. Put a check in the column where the statement applies.

Statements	Actual Sin	Original Sin	Iniquity
1. It is the breaking of God's commandments.			
2. It is a weakness or gravitation in our nature for certain sins.			
3. It is the result of Adam's sin.			
4. We can be forgiven by confessing it and asking for forgiveness.			
5. It is the total corruption of our nature that seeks to be independent of God.			
6. My conscience tells me not to do something, but I do it anyway.			
7. It can be forgiven by the blood of Jesus.			
8. I know what is right to do, but I don't do it.			
9. I have a problem with stealing. Even when I determine not to steal, I still steal.			
10. It is the reason why man has an innate enmity against God.			
11. It is the result of my willful and continual breaking of God's commandments or inherited from our ancestors.			

CHAPTER 16-19: UNDERSTANDING THE FIRST – FOURTH COMMANDMENTS

Activity: Man's Relationship With God

Provide two examples of disobedience and then two examples of obedience for each commandment listed below.

Commandment	Examples of Disobedience	Example of Obedience
You shall have no other gods before me.		
You shall not make a carved (graven) image.		
You shall not take the name of the LORD your God in vain.		
Remember the Sabbath day, to keep it holy.		

- 27 -

CHAPTER 16-19: UNDERSTANDING THE FIRST - FOURTH COMMANDMENTS

Activity: Expand The Meaning Of The Third And Fourth Commandments

Using The Bible and the *UNDERSTANDING GOD* book, examine how the meanings of these two commandments are expanded in the New Testament.

```
┌─────────────────────────────────────┐
│  You shall not take the name of the  │
│        LORD your God in vain.        │
└─────────────────────────────────────┘
```

Meaning of this commandment   Meaning of this commandment
      in the Old Covenant   in the New Covenant

```
┌──────────────────┐          ┌──────────────────┐
│                  │          │                  │
│                  │          │                  │
│                  │          │                  │
│                  │          │                  │
└──────────────────┘          └──────────────────┘
```

```
┌─────────────────────────────────────┐
│  Remember the Sabbath day to keep it holy.  │
└─────────────────────────────────────┘
```

Meaning of this commandment   Meaning of this commandment
      in the Old Covenant   in the New Covenant

```
┌──────────────────┐          ┌──────────────────┐
│                  │          │                  │
│                  │          │                  │
│                  │          │                  │
│                  │          │                  │
└──────────────────┘          └──────────────────┘
```

What makes the 4th Commandment unique among all the commandments?

Resource Scriptures: Mark 2: 27-28.

CHAPTER 20-25: UNDERSTANDING THE TEN COMMANDMENTS
Activity: Applying Your Knowledge

For each of the statements below, mark the commandment or commandments that are being broken.

	1st	2nd	3rd	4th	5th	6th	7th	8th	9th	10th
I know my mother is elderly, but I don't think I should have to make sure she is taken care of. She and dad should have planned ahead.										
Whenever my friend gets angry, he swears.										
Money, money, money. If only I had money, all my problems would disappear.										
I told the police officer I was late for a flight and that was why I was speeding. I was really on my way to lunch.										
My new car is a beauty. Nobody is going to drive it except me. I've spent all week waxing and shining it.										
In the paper today, I read a man shot and killed his wife.										
It's only a pack of mints. This store can afford the loss.										
My neighbor had an affair with another woman. You would understand if you ever met his wife – a difficult person to deal with!										
My brother works and works. He never has time to pray or even go to church with his family.										
John just got a brand new Harley motorcycle. Now every one of my friends has a Harley except me. I hope his motorcycle turns out to be a lemon!										
I got an award my co-worker wanted. When it was announced, he called me names that cut to the heart.										
The couple next door is living together but they are not married.										
Tom wants to do things his way all the time. He doesn't like anyone telling him what to do.										
Fame! Fame! All Meghan cares about is becoming a famous celebrity.										

CHAPTER 20 - 25: UNDERSTANDING THE FIFTH – TENTH COMMANDMENTS

Activity: Can You Match It?

Match the statements below to each of the Ten Commandments.

_____ 1. You must obey and respect your parents.

_____ 2. Take time to worship and praise God, to "rest" in Him.

_____ 3. God must come first in your life.

_____ 4. You must respect life.

_____ 5. You must tell the truth. You must speak well of your family and friends.

_____ 6. You must respect the property and possessions of others.

_____ 7. You must be thankful for what God has given you and be pleased when He blesses others.

_____ 8. You must praise the name of the Lord.

_____ 9. You must worship God in spirit and in truth.

_____ 10. You must be faithful in marriage.

---

1. You shall have no other gods before me.
2. You shall not make any carved (graven) images.
3. You shall not take the name of the LORD in vain.
4. Remember the Sabbath, to keep it holy.
5. Honor your father and your mother.
6. You shall not kill (murder).
7. You shall not commit adultery.
8. You shall not steal.
9. You shall be bear false witness against your neighbor.
10. You shall not covet.

Chapter 20 - 25: UNDERSTANDING THE FIFTH – TENTH COMMANDMENTS

Activity: Turn It Around

Most of the commandments tell us what *not* to do. Rewrite the commandments so they tell us what we *should* do. Commandments 4 and 5 are exceptions. They do not begin with "You shall *not*." Restate these two commandments in your own words.

1. You shall have no other gods before me.

2. You shall not make any carved (graven) images.

3. You shall not take the name of the LORD your God in vain.

4. Remember the Sabbath day, to keep it holy.

5. Honor your father and your mother.

6. You shall not kill (murder).

7. You shall not commit adultery.

8. You shall not steal.

9. You shall not bear false witness against your neighbor.

10. You shall not covet.

CHAPTER 26: UNDERSTANDING SALVATION

Activity: Doctrines Of Christ

Sometimes the terminology we find in The Bible is difficult to understand. Try to match the terms of the Doctrines of Christ with the correct definition.

_____ 1. Repentance from Dead Works

_____ 2. Faith Toward God

_____ 3. Doctrine of Baptisms

_____ 4. Laying on of Hands

_____ 5. Resurrection of the Dead

_____ 6. Eternal Judgment

A. An anointed believer can impart to us divine gifts and abilities.

B. We are joined to Christ's death, burial and resurrection; we receive the Gift of the Holy Spirit.

C. We realize we can't earn salvation by doing good works.

D. We believe Christ is coming again and there is eternal life.

E. We believe the blood of Jesus can forgive our sins and make us "right" with God.

F. We have to answer whether or not we have accepted Jesus as our Savior. We receive reward or punishment for how we have lived our lives on earth.

CHAPTER 27: UNDERSTANDING THE REPENTANCE FROM DEAD WORKS

Activity: Earning Salvation?

Salvation is a gift of God, yet man sometimes feels that salvation needs to be earned. Read the following statements and determine if it is God's Way or Man's Way.

God's Way	Man's Way	
		1. I go to church every Sunday because I feel it will make me worthy of God's favor.
		2. If I try really hard to be very good, I can make myself worthy of God's grace.
		3. I accept that Jesus died as a sacrifice for my sins.
		4. I admit I have broken God's commandments and am a sinner.
		5. I give my tithes and offering to the church so God will know that I deserve His gift of salvation.
		6. I pray certain prayers three times a day to show God that I am good enough to be saved.
		7. I believe there is nothing I can do to earn my salvation.
		8. People who are basically good – give to the poor, help the needy, aren't a detriment to society - should be the ones who receive God's gift of salvation.

CHAPTER 28: UNDERSTANDING FAITH TOWARD GOD

Activity: Fact Or Fiction

Determine if the following statements are fact or fiction.

<u>FACT</u>   <u>FICTION</u>

_____   _____   1. Faith is a gift from God.

_____   _____   2. God justifies us by exchanging our guilt and sin for Christ's righteousness.

_____   _____   3. God creates faith in us as we hear God's Word preached, taught or as we read the Scriptures.

_____   _____   4. God justifies those who are trying to be good.

_____   _____   5. It is the Holy Spirit who convicts and convinces us that we are sinners.

_____   _____   6. If we sincerely confess our sins, Jesus will forgive our sins by His blood.

_____   _____   7. Genuine repentance for our sins is demonstrated by real change in our lives.

_____   _____   8. To appreciate the work of justification, we must truly believe we are sinners.

_____   _____   9. The only time we need to confess our sins is when we accept Jesus as our Savior.

_____   _____   10. Once I have accepted Jesus as my Savior, I am free to live my life as I please.

Why wouldn't God make it harder for us to be saved? After all, it was not easy for Jesus to make the way of salvation available to man.

CHAPTER 29: UNDERSTANDING WATER BAPTISM

Activity: If You Were The Teacher!

Imagine you are the teacher. What do you think are the most important points students should understand about Water Baptism?

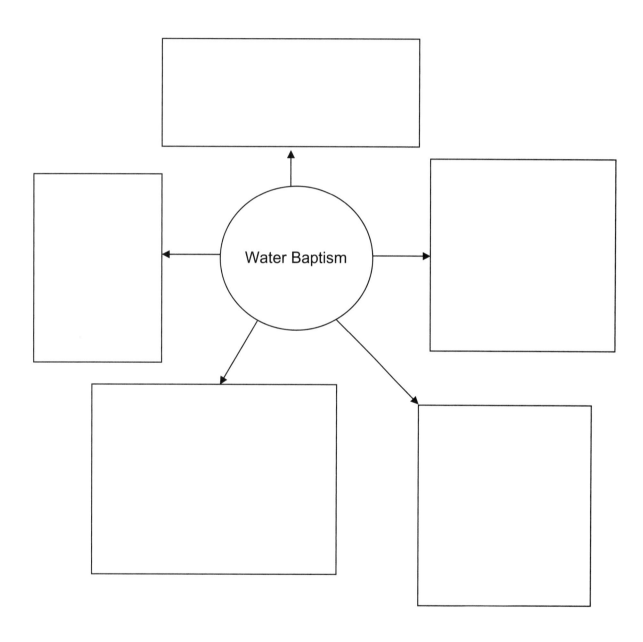

CHAPTER 30: UNDERSTANDING THE HOLY SPIRIT

Activity: Agree Or Disagree

Decide whether you agree or disagree with the statements about the Holy Spirit. Be prepared to explain your answer.

Agree	Disagree	
		1. The Holy Spirit is the second person of the Holy Tri-Unity.
		2. The Holy Spirit is all-powerful, all-knowing, everywhere, and eternal.
		3. The Holy Spirit comforts, intercedes, leads, strengthens, and equips the believer.
		4. The Holy Spirit deals with believers only.
		5. Creation was only the work of the Holy Spirit.
		6. The Holy Spirit is the author of the Scriptures.
		7. The Holy Spirit raised Jesus from the dead.
		8. It is the Holy Spirit who reveals truth to us.
		9. The Holy Spirit should be to us what Jesus was to His disciples.
		10. Blasphemy against the Holy Spirit can be forgiven if the person repents.

CHAPTER 31: UNDERSTANDING THE BAPTISM OF THE HOLY SPIRIT

Activity: The Blessings Of The Holy Spirit

Using the Scriptures below, write a significant truth about the Holy Spirit.

Scripture	Truth
Acts 1:8 Luke 24:49	
2 Cor. 3:18	
John 16:13	
Acts 13:2	
1 Cor. 12:4-11	
Acts 2:17	
Luke 11:9-13	
Rom. 8:26	
1 Cor. 14:2	
1 Cor. 14:4 Jude 1:20	
1 Cor. 12:12-13	

CHAPTER 32: UNDERSTANDING THE BAPTISM OF THE HOLY SPIRIT

Activity: Conforming To His Image

Match the following Scriptures to the statements that best paraphrase their meaning.

_____ 1. Rom. 8:29

_____ 2. Eph. 4:22-24

_____ 3. Heb. 12:7-8

_____ 4. Heb. 12:10

_____ 5. Isa. 48:10

_____ 6. Phil. 3:12

_____ 7. Gal. 5:25

_____ 8. 2 Cor. 7:1

A. Allow the Holy Spirit to lead us in every part of our life, in every aspect of our walk.

B. When we are chastened or corrected by God, it is proof to us that we are indeed sons of God and He is our Father.

C. I am not perfect, but I must keep working to be all that Christ saved me for and wants me to become.

D. We are refined and perfected by God through the difficult times and situations we experience in our lives.

E. We must throw off our old habits and ways. Our attitudes, our way of thinking must be changed for the better. We must put on the new nature, created in the image of God's righteousness and holiness.

F. Since God has given to us great promises, let's turn away from everything in our live that is wrong or corrupt, purifying ourselves in reverence to God.

G. From the beginning God knew who would come to Him and become like His Son, conforming to the image of Christ.

H. God's chastening is always right and for our best that we may share His Holiness.

CHAPTER 33: UNDERSTANDING THE LAYING ON OF HANDS

Activity: What Does the Bible Say?

Use the Scriptures given to fill in the chart below.

Scripture	Who is laying hands for impartation?	Who is having hands laid on them?	What was imparted?
Deut. 34:9			
Gen. 48:14, 20			
Luke 4:40			
Mark 10:16			
Acts 28:8			
Mark 17:17-18			
Acts 19:6			
Acts 15:32			
Acts 13:1-3			
Rom. 1:11			

CHAPTER 34: UNDERSTANDING THE RESURRECTION OF THE DEAD

Activity: What Will Happen?

First attempt to fill in the blanks without using the *UNDERSTANDING GOD* book, then check your answers using the textbook. Make changes as needed.

1. When a believer dies his body decays and returns to dust, but his soul and spirit

   return to _____.

2. The _____ of the body then lies dormant awaiting resurrection.

3. The soul and the spirit of the righteous dead are located in God's presence in

   heaven called _____.

4. The souls of the wicked dead abide in _____.

5. At the First Resurrection all those "in" Christ, whether alive or resurrected, shall

   receive a new, immortal, spiritual _____.

6. The Second Resurrection will occur after the reign of Christ on _____ ,

   and is the resurrection of the _____ dead.

7. All who reject Christ shall be sentenced to _____ again.

   Their soul and _____ will be cast into a place of eternal torment called

   _____ .

8. Their bodies will die again because _____ is promised only to

   believers.

- 40 -

CHAPTER 35: UNDERSTANDING ETERNAL JUDGMENT

Activity: Two Judgments

Determine how these Judgments are similar to and different from each other.

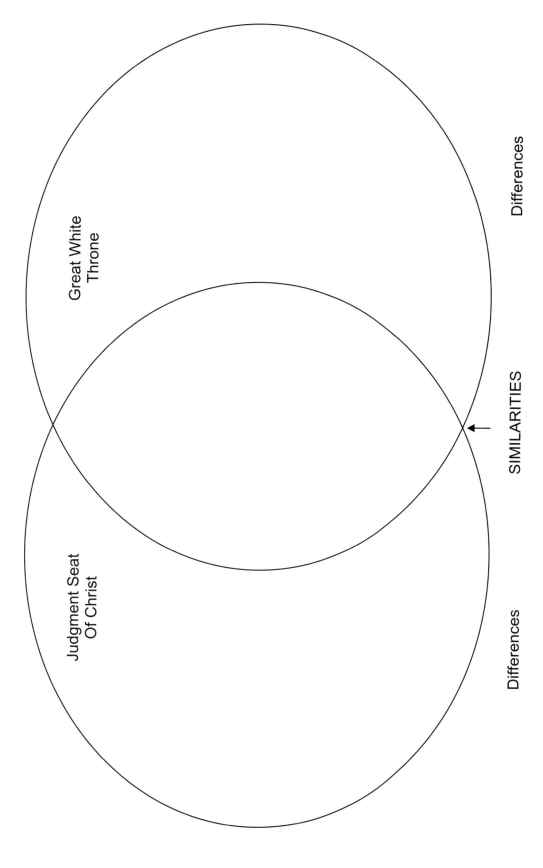

Great White
Throne

Judgment Seat
Of Christ

SIMILARITIES

Differences

Differences

CHAPTER 35: UNDERSTANDING ETERNAL JUDGMENT

Activity: Which One Or Both?

Read the following statements and determine if the statement applies to the Judgment Seat of Christ (the First Judgment) or the Great White Throne Judgment (the Second Judgment).

Judgment Seat of Christ	Great White Throne Judgment	Statements
		1. This is a judgment of believers.
		2. This is the judgment for those who are part of the First Resurrection.
		3. This judgment takes place after Jesus returns to earth.
		4. It is believed this judgment takes place after Jesus reigns on earth 1,000 years.
		5. Jesus Christ will be the Judge at this judgment.
		6. This is a judgment of unbelievers.
		7. Record books will be used at this judgment in determining a person's eternal destiny.

CHAPTER 36: UNDERSTANDING THE APOSTLES' CREED

Activity: Interpret The Creed

Rewrite the Apostles' Creed without changing its meaning.

1. I believe in God the Father Almighty, creator of heaven and earth;

2. and in Jesus Christ, His only Son, our Lord;

3. who was conceived by the Holy Ghost,

4. born of the Virgin Mary,

5. suffered under Pontius Pilate,

6. was crucified, died and was buried.

7. He descended into hell,

8. the third day He arose again from the dead;

9. He ascended into heaven,

10. sitteth at the right hand of God, the Father Almighty;

11. from thence He shall come to judge the living and the dead.

12. I believe in the Holy Ghost, the Holy Christian Church,

13. the communion of saints, the forgiveness of sins

14. the resurrection of the dead and life everlasting. Amen.

CHAPTER 37: UNDERSTANDING CHRIST'S CHURCH

Activity: Fact Or Fiction

Determine if the following statements are fact or fiction:

Fact	Fiction	Statements
		1. The Church is referred to as the Body of Christ.
		2. The Church is a spiritual nation made up of the people of God.
		3. Christ's Church is located in a temple in Jerusalem.
		4. The Church is referred to as the Bride of Christ.
		5. Once we are water baptized, we automatically become members of Christ's Church.
		6. The proof we are truly members of Christ's Church is our ability to love other Christians with compassion and understanding.
		7. Racial, social, and gender barriers are not to exist in Christ's Church.
		8. Being a member of Christ's Church depends on your natural birth.
		9. Christ's Church is a universal church.
		10. The word "church" means "called out ones" not a "called out building."

CHAPTER 38: UNDERSTANDING THE LOCAL CHURCH

Activity: Benefits and Responsibilities

Brainstorm the benefits and responsibilities of being a member of a Local Church.

Benefits of Being a Member of a Local Church	Responsibilities of a Member of a Local Church

Why do so many people want the benefits of a Local Church but struggle with the responsibilities?

CHAPTER 39: UNDERSTANDING WORSHIP

Activity: Old Covenant And New Covenant Worship

Identify the difference and similarities between the Old Covenant and New Covenant worship.

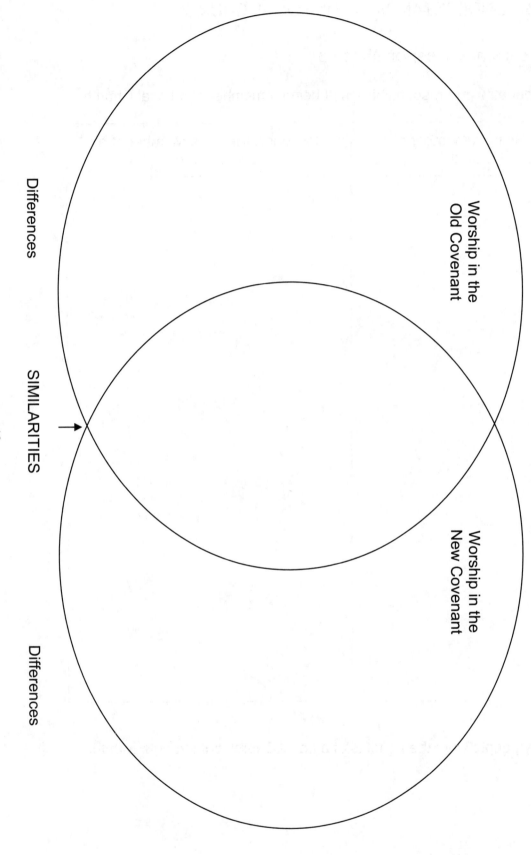

Worship in the
Old Covenant

Worship in the
New Covenant

Differences

SIMILARITIES

Differences

CHAPTER 39: UNDERSTANDING WORSHIP

Activity: Temples Of Worship

The meaning of a "temple of God" in the New Covenant differs from its meaning in the Old Covenant. Read the Scriptures below. What lessons about the "temple of God" and worship can we learn from these Scriptures?

Questions	Old Testament Temple of God 2 Chronicles 5:13-14 2 Chronicles 7:1-3	New Testament Temple of God 1 Corinthians 3:16-17 1 Corinthians 6:19-20
1. Describe the temple of God based on these Scriptures.		
2. Lessons to be learned from the Old and New Testament about worship and the temple of God.		

CHAPTER 39: UNDERSTANDING WORSHIP

Activity: Forms Of Worship

We are to worship God with our bodies, our lips, and our service. Provide examples of each.

Forms of Worship	Examples
Bodies	
Lips	
Service	

CHAPTER 40: UNDERSTANDING PRAYER AND FASTING

Activity: The Lord's Prayer

The Lord's Prayer provides a pattern for praying. "Translate" each phrase of this prayer into today's language. What does each part of the prayer instruct us to do as we pray?

1. Our Father which art in heaven, hallowed be thy name.

2. Thy kingdom come, thy will be done in earth, as it is in heaven.

3. Give us this day our daily bread.

4. And forgive us our debts, as we forgive our debtors.

5. And lead us not into temptation, but deliver us from evil;

6. For thine is the kingdom, and the power, and the glory forever. Amen.

CHAPTER 40: UNDERSTANDING P RAYER AND FASTING

Activity: Learning To Pray

The Bible states we can pray not only for our own personal needs but also for the needs of others. We can intercede for the needs in our world, our community, our church, our families. In the categories listed below, write specific needs for which we can pray.

Government Authorities	
World Needs	
Church Needs (members who have needs)	
People at your work, school or community who have a need	
Family Needs	
Personal Needs	

CHAPTER 40: UNDERSTANDING PRAYER AND FASTING

Activity: What The Bible Says

Turn to the Scriptures below and learn what The Bible says about prayer and fasting.

Scripture	Truths
Phil. 4:6	
Mark 11:24	
1 John 5:14-15	
James 4:3	
Mark 11:25-26	
Eph. 6:18	
1 Peter 3:7	
Rom. 8:2-27	
1 Cor. 14:15	
Matt. 5:44	
Ezra 8:23 Isa. 58:6 Dan. 9:3	

CHAPTER 41: UNDERSTANDING THE GIFTS OF THE HOLY SPIRIT

Activity: The Gifts Of The Holy Spirit

Sometimes the terminology we find in The Bible is difficult to understand. Try to match the term with its definition.

_____ 1. Gift of Faith

_____ 2. Gift of Miracles

_____ 3. Gift of Healing

_____ 4. Gift of Prophecy

_____ 5. Gift of Tongues

_____ 6. Gift of the Interpretation of Tongues

_____ 7. Word of Wisdom

_____ 8. Word of Knowledge

_____ 9. Gift of Discerning of spirits

A. Being able to pray for the sick and they are healed.

B. Being able to perceive the true spirit of a person.

C. Being able to understand and explain the meaning of divinely inspired words.

D. Being given a divine answer to a difficult problem or situation.

E. Being given the ability to change events and circumstances or to interfere with nature by the supernatural power of God.

F. Being able to speak divinely inspired words which can be understood by another.

G. Having the ability to believe and to act on what you cannot see.

H. Being able to speak Holy Spirit inspired words of encouragement, direction, and comfort to the church.

I. Being able to know facts or details about a situation or person without having been told by someone.

CHAPTER 42: UNDERSTANDING THE MINISTRIES OF THE HOLY SPIRIT

Activity: Inventory Of Gifts/Abilities

Respond as best you can to the statements below.

1   List your natural talents and/or interests.

2. List any spiritual gifts or abilities God has given you. If you are not aware of any, then list the spiritual gifts or abilities you desire.

3. How could your spiritual and/or natural abilities or interests be used in an area of service/ministry in your church?

CHAPTER 42: UNDERSTANDING THE MINISTRIES OF THE HOLY SPIRIT

Activity: Scenarios

How would you respond to the following people? Your advice, though, must be based on Biblical principles.

1. I would like to find a place of ministry in my church, but I won't get involved until God tells me through a prophetic word what ministry He has called me to.

2. I am a teacher by profession. I have a gift to teach, and I want to use that gift in my church. I think I will call the pastor today. I'll tell him he needs to get a class together for me so I can fulfill my ministry of teaching.

3. If it's God's will for me to have a ministry in my church, then someone will personally invite me to get involved. Until then, I think it is best to just attend services.

4. My good friend doesn't have just one ministry; she has many. She is a gifted soloist, teaches the young adults, and speaks at women's retreats. I send cards to the sick and elderly. I'm sure my ministry isn't nearly as valuable to God as hers are.

CHAPTER 42: UNDERSTANDING THE MINISTRIES OF THE HOLY SPIRIT

Activity: Defining Areas Of Ministry

Use the *UNDERSTANDING GOD* book to help define what is involved in the ministries listed below:

MINISTRY	WHAT DOES THIS MINISTRY INVOLVE?
APOSTLE	
PROPHET	
EVANGELIST	
PASTOR	
TEACHER	
GOVERNMENTS	
HELPS	

Provide examples of the following ministries:

MINISTRY	EXAMPLES OF THIS MINISTRY
GOVERNMENTS	
HELPS	

CHAPTER 43: UNDERSTANDING THE SACRAMENTS OF THE CHURCH

Activity: What Do You Think You Know?

A sacrament consists of an outward experience that is accompanied by an inner spiritual work. Except for the Sacrament of Water Baptism, the following sacraments have not been studied. So, *what do you think* are the outward experience and inner spiritual work of each of these sacraments?

SACRAMENTS	Outward Experience	Inner Spiritual Work
Water Baptism		
Lord's Supper		
Footwashing		
Anointing with Oil		
Confirmation		
Matrimony		
Presentation of a Child to God		

CHAPTER 44: UNDERSTANDING THE LORD'S SUPPER

Activity: Turning To The Bible

Read the Scriptures below, and then answer the following two questions:

SCRIPTURES	WHAT DOES THIS SCRIPTURE SAY CONCERNING THE LORD'S SUPPER?	HOW DOES THIS APPLY TO YOU PERSONALLY?
Luke 22:17-20		
1 Corinthians 11:25		
John 6:51-53		
1 Corinthians 11:26		
Exodus 13:16-17		
1 Corinthians 11:28-29		

CHAPTER 44: UNDERSTANDING THE LORD'S SUPPER

Activity: The Passover And The Lord's Supper

Identify the differences and similarities between The Lord's Supper and the Old Covenant Passover.

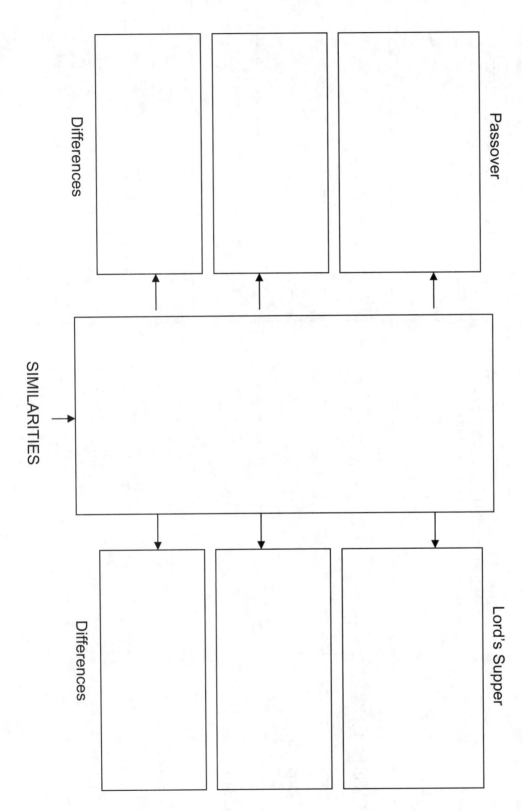

Passover

Differences

SIMILARITIES

Differences

Lord's Supper

CHAPTER 45: UNDERSTANDING FOOTWASHING

Activity: Nick Needs To Know

Nick is a member of your class. He has a lot of questions about the Sacrament of Footwashing. Using the Bible and your *UNDERSTANDING GOD* book, answer Nick's questions.

1. Why did Jesus wash His disciples' feet?

2. Isn't this sacrament just meant for Jesus' disciples?

3. How do we know this sacrament is still meant to be administered today?

4. Why can't we just substitute washing hands instead of feet?

5. What will Footwashing really accomplish?

6. How can washing feet cause a spiritual work to take place in my heart?

7. How do I know if I need this sacrament?

8. What do I do while someone is washing my feet?

9. What do I pray for as I wash someone's feet?

CHAPTER 45: UNDERSTANDING FOOTWASHING

Activity: Fact Or Fiction

Determine if the following statements are fact or fiction.

FACT   FICTION

_____ _____ 1. This sacrament reveals to us that to be a partner with Christ we need to be servants of all.

_____ _____ 2. Jesus instituted this sacrament after His resurrection.

_____ _____ 3. The disciples needed this sacrament because they were arguing among themselves about who would have the greatest position in God's Kingdom.

_____ _____ 4. The outward experience of this sacrament only involves someone washing our feet.

_____ _____ 5. In this sacrament God deals with our innate desire to rule over others and to exalt ourselves at the expense of others.

_____ _____ 6. We can experience the spiritual work of this sacrament without having to wash feet, if we just have faith to receive it.

_____ _____ 7. We can substitute washing hands instead of washing feet.

_____ _____ 8. There is a gift of love for one another that we receive in this sacrament that makes it possible for us to be genuine servants of Christ.

_____ _____ 9. This sacrament helps maintain unity in the church.

_____ _____ 10. You will only need to participate in this sacrament one time.

Why would Jesus establish the washing of feet as the outward experience of this sacrament?

CHAPTER 46: UNDERSTANDING HEALING AND ANOINTING WITH OIL

Activity: Common Denominators

Read the following Scriptures that document healings by Jesus. Answer the questions below, and then determine the common denominators of these healings.

Scriptures	Who needed healing?	What was the need?	How was the healing administered ?
Matt. 8:5-13			
Matt. 9:20-22			
Matt. 9:27-29			
Luke 5:17-25			

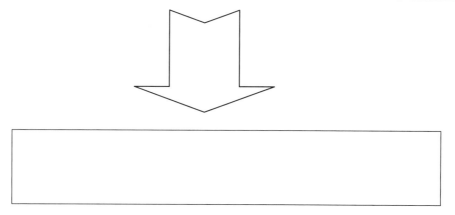

Common Denominators

CHAPTER 46: UNDERSTANDING HEALING AND ANOINTING WITH OIL

Connector Activity: Fill It In

Use the UNDERSTANDING GOD book and what you have learned about divine healing and the Sacrament of Anointing with Oil to complete the following sentences.

1. The outward experience of this sacrament is being anointed with _____ .

2. The inner spiritual work of this sacrament is _____ and restoration.

3. This sacrament is for the healing of the body, soul or _____ .

4. We must have _____ when we pray for healing.

5. The oil symbolizes the presence of the _____ .

6. The Sacrament of Anointing with Oil is administered by the _____ of the

   church.

7. Before this sacrament is administered we need to examine ourselves.

   • Do we have a(n) _____ spirit?

   • Are we robbing God of our _____ and offerings?

   • Are we harboring _____ toward another believer?

8. The Sacrament of Anointing with Oil is primarily for the healing and _____

   of the soul.

CHAPTER 47: UNDERSTANDING CONFIRMATION

Activity: Fact Or Fiction

Determine if the following statements are fact or fiction.

FACT   FICTION

_____   _____   1. This sacrament is optional.

_____   _____   2. This sacrament was practiced by the Apostles in the
                               Early Christian Church.

_____   _____   3. Once a believer has accepted Jesus Christ as Savior,
                               he/she is ready for this sacrament.

_____   _____   4. The outward experience of this sacrament is when a
                               believer kneels and asks Jesus to confirm him/her.

_____   _____   5. This sacrament establishes a believer's faith in Jesus
                               Christ so he/she can face the difficulties of life and not
                               become discouraged and defeated.

_____   _____   6. This sacrament establishes a believer's faith so he/she
                               can become a mature Christian.

_____   _____   7. This sacrament brings strength to the Church.

_____   _____   8. Children can be confirmed as infants.

For any answer that is "fiction," turn it into a "fact."

- 63 -

CHAPTER 48: UNDERSTANDING MATRIMONY

Activity: Roles Of The Husband and Wife

Identify the differences and similarities between the roles of the husband and wife.

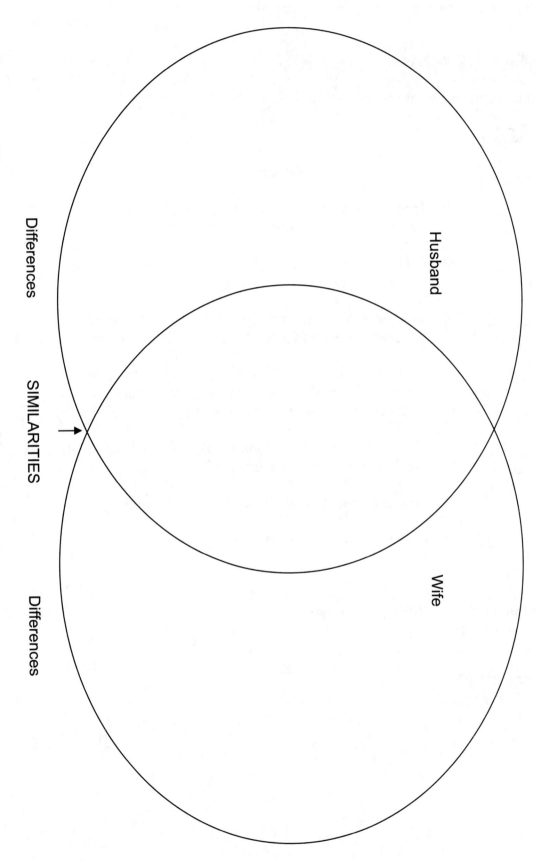

Husband

Wife

Differences

SIMILARITIES

Differences

CHAPTER 48: UNDERSTANDING MATRIMONY

Activity: Scenarios

These people have problems concerning marriage. You are the marriage counselor. Give them good advice based upon what The Bible says about marriage.

1. Megan:

    "Jason and I want to get married. I'm a Christian, but he is not. That doesn't really matter, does it? After all, we're compatible in every other way. And really, it is love that matters and love will conquer all."

2. Joe:

    "Nicole and I really hit it off. I've never been in love like this before. I want to marry her, but I have some financial baggage that I don't want to saddle her with. If we get married, she will be liable for my debts. I don't want that but at the same time, I know she is the one. We've decided we will just live with each other. That way it gives me time to work out my financial problems."

3. Lauren:

    "Owen and I have been married for a couple of years. We really love each other but lately we're struggling. Owen's mother just won't leave us alone. She is always butting into our affairs and Owen always goes to her with his problems instead of me? Sometimes I feel like he loves her more than me."

CHAPTER 48: UNDERSTANDING MATRIMONY

4. Evan:

"My parents divorced when I was 10. My aunt and uncle are divorced. My cousin and his wife are divorced. I really love Dominque but I am absolutely terrified that if we marry, we will end up divorced as well. It doesn't seem like anyone in my family can stay committed. Maybe it would be best if Dominque and I just lived together. God has to like that better than divorce!"

5. Abigail:

"My husband read in The Bible that he is the head of the family. Now he is acting like he is the King of England. He is constantly giving me orders and treats me like I'm his servant. Is this what The Bible means when it says the husband is the head?"

CHAPTER 49: UNDERSTANDING THE PRESENTATION OF A CHILD TO GOD

Activity: Family Responsibilities

God has established an order for the Christian family. There are responsibilities for both parents and children. Determine whether the following responsibilities belong to the Father (F), the Mother (M), Both (B), Children (C), All (A).

_____   1. To pray for the family.

_____   2. To be united in spiritual leadership for the family.

_____   3. To be the vital link between your spouse and the children.

_____   4. To acknowledge Christ is the center of the home.

_____   5. To attend church regularly.

_____   6. To establish an order of discipline in the home.

_____   7. To teach the children to love and worship God.

_____   8. To be obedient.

_____   9. To care for them when they are elderly.

_____   10. To honor them by the way we talk to them and about them.

_____   11. To help them discover their talents and fulfill their divine purpose.

_____   12. To ensure they receive the necessary instruction to lay a solid spiritual foundation in the Doctrines of Christ.

_____   13. To teach them how to be givers.

_____   14. To be held responsible for the spiritual and physical welfare of the family.

_____   15. To teach them to love and trust the Lord.

_____   16. To discipline with love and patience.

CHAPTER 50: UNDERSTANDING GIVING

Activity: Principles of Giving

Using The Bible, identify the principles of giving that bring blessing to our lives.

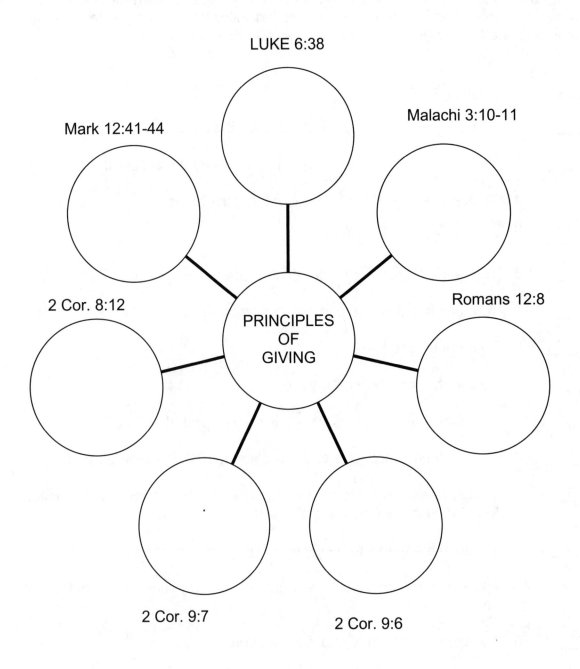

CHAPTER 50: UNDERSTANDING GIVING

Activity: God's Way Versus Man's Way

The following statements deal with the principles of giving. Decide which statements reflect the way man wants to give and which statements reflect the way God wants us to give.

God's Way	Man's Way	
		1. I give my tithe to my church because I'm afraid God will zap me if I don't.
		2. I give my tithe to my church because I understand that God is my source.
		3. Giving cheerfully and willingly is a way to store up eternal treasure in heaven.
		4. I give my tithe. That's enough. Don't ask me to give to anyone or anything else.
		5. We are to give to the poor.
		6. I don't mind giving, but I think the people I give to should at least thank me.
		7. I'll tithe off the net of my income. After all, that's the amount I have to live on.
		8. I consider paying my tithe a bill I owe God.
		9. I can give of my time instead of my tithe.
		10. I give of my time and talents as well as my finances.

Activity: The Pattern for Resolving Problems

Tom has been teaching Sunday school in the same room for ten years. The Sunday school director assigned Joan to teach a new class in the room next door. When Tom arrives Sunday, his portable whiteboard is missing. He goes into Joan's room and sees an identical whiteboard. He asks Joan where she got the board. "I requested it from the office," she replied. Tom left her room muttering under his breath. Joan is offended because she thinks Tom thinks she has "stolen" his whiteboard. Using Matthew 18:15-17, how should this situation be resolved?

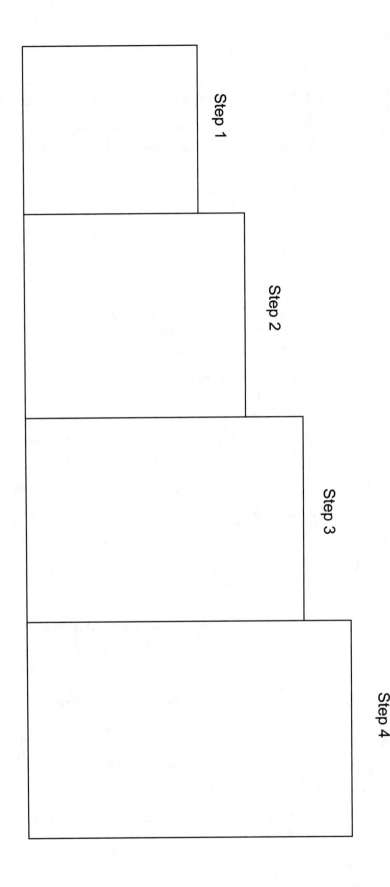

Step 1

Step 2

Step 3

Step 4

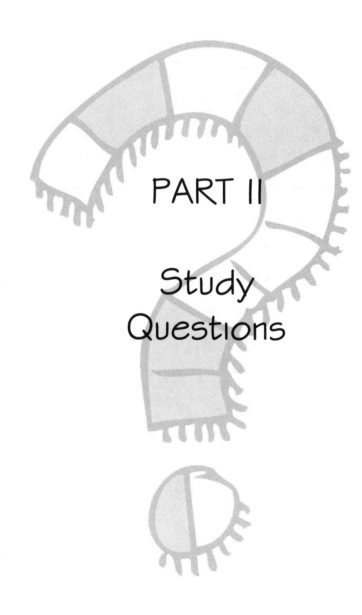

PART II

Study
Questions

CHAPTER 1: UNDERSTANDING GOD

1. What is the triune name of our triune God?

2. Describe how the three identities of God operated in unity to:

    a. Save us? (Read 1 Peter 1:2)

    b. Resurrect Jesus? (Read Rom. 1:4)

3. How can God be triune – God the Father, God the Son, God the Holy Spirit?

4. What attribute of God do you find most intriguing or interesting? Why?

5. How does our understanding of God affect the way we live our lives?

CHAPTER 2: UNDERSTANDING THE BIBLE

1. What makes the Bible unique among all other "holy" (religious) books?

2. Read 2 Timothy 3:15. What is the primary reason we were given the Bible?

3. Read 2 Timothy 3:16. List three more reasons the Bible was given to us.

   a.

   b.

   c.

4. What is the difference between the Old Testament and the New Testament?

5. Why do we need to ask the Holy Spirit to help us when we read the Bible?

Name: _____

Date: _____

CHAPTER 3: UNDERSTANDING THE SPIRIT WORLD

1. List three characteristics of angels which are different from man and three characteristics of angels that are the similar to man?

Differences	Similarities
a)	a)
b)	b)
c)	c)

2. Give four ways angels minister to us today:

    a.

    b.

    c.

    d.

3. Hebrews 1:14 states that angels minister to those who are "heirs of salvation." So if there are angels who are to those who are believers, why aren't we more aware of their existence and interventions in our lives? (Hint: Rev. 22:8-9)

4. What was Lucifer's sin?

5. What will eventually happen to Satan and his demons?

- 78 -

CHAPTER 4: UNDERSTANDING CREATION

1. Describe what God created on each day:

Day 1	Day 2	Day 3	Day 4	Day 5	Day 6

2. What does it mean to be made in the "image and likeness" of God?

3. Describe how man was created. Describe how woman was created.

4. Read Genesis Chapters 1 and 2. Why did God create Adam and Eve? List at least three reasons.

   •

   •

   •

5. What are the flaws in the Theory of Evolution?

6. Why are people willing to put their faith in evolution as the answer to our existence, rather than in God as the Creator?

CHAPTER 5: UNDERSTANDING GOD'S COVENANT WITH MAN

1. What is the difference between a covenant man makes with man and a covenant God makes with man?

2. Name the six covenants God established with man.

   a)

   b)

   c)

   d)

   e)

   f)

3. Why did God make these covenants with man?

4. What do you think are the benefits of being in covenant with God?

CHAPTER 6: UNDERSTANDING GOD'S COVENANT WITH ADAM

1. What did God require of Adam and Eve in this covenant He established with them?

2. Why did God put the Tree of Knowledge of Good and Evil in the Garden of Eden?

3. Why did Adam and Eve eat of the Tree of Knowledge of Good and Evil?

   d) How was Adam's sin similar to Lucifer's sin?

   e) Why was God so angry with Adam and Eve?

   f) How did Adam react to God when he was caught in sin?

   g) In what ways do we see ourselves in the actions and reactions of Adam and Eve?

CHAPTER 7: UNDERSTANDING GOD'S COVENANT WITH NOAH

1. How was Noah able to remain righteous in the midst of a corrupt world?

2. What were the terms of the covenant God established with Noah?

God would:	If Noah would:

3. Why did God decide to destroy life on earth with a flood?

4. What lessons can we learn from Noah?

5. After mankind's fresh beginning with Noah and his family, how could mankind once again rebel against God's command to multiply and fill the earth?

6. Why did God stop the building of the Tower of Babel?

Name: _____

Date: _____

CHAPTER 8: UNDERSTANDING GOD'S COVENANT WITH ABRAHAM

1. Read Genesis 12:1-3. What were the promises God made to Abraham in this covenant?

2. What did God require of Abraham in order for the promises of this covenant to be fulfilled?

3. Why was the sign of the circumcision so important to this covenant?

4. Read Genesis 22:1-18. Why did God test Abraham by asking him to sacrifice his son, Isaac?

5. What important lessons can we learn from Abraham and his relationship with God? Hint: Read Genesis 18:17-19 and James 2:23.

6. Though which son and grandson was this Abrahamic Covenant passed?

   a. Son:

   b. Grandson:

- 88 -

CHAPTER 9: UNDERSTANDING GOD'S COVENANT WITH MOSES

1. What was Moses like when God met him at the burning bush?

2. How did Moses become such a great leader?

3. How did God prove to the Israelites that He was greater than the most powerful nation on earth – the Egyptians?

4. Why did God want Moses to take the Israelites to Mt. Sinai?

5. What were the terms of the Mosaic Covenant?

God would:	If the Nation of Israel would:

6. Why were the Ten Commandments given to Moses and the nation of Israel?

CHAPTER 10: UNDERSTANDING GOD'S COVENANT WITH DAVID

1. Why did David have such a special relationship with God?

2. David became king of Israel. However, his journey to becoming king was not filled with great difficulties. What did David learn during this period of his life?

3. What did David do that prompted God to establish a covenant with him?

4. What were the covenant promises God made with David?

5. Which descendant of David established his throne forever?

6. David was not a perfect man. David failed God by committing murder and adultery. Although God forgave David, what were the consequences of his sin?

7. What lessons can we learn from David and his covenant relationship with God?

CHAPTER 11: UNDERSTANDING JESUS CHRIST

1. Jesus never claimed a geographical or political kingdom. He didn't sit on a throne or live in a palace. How do we know then that He was indeed a king, in fact an eternal king?

2. How do we know that the power of the Kingdom of God is real?

3. What are the teachings of the God's Kingdom?

4. How did Jesus prove He truly was the Son of God?

5. How do we enter into the Kingdom of God?

6. Do you believe Jesus is truly the Son of God? Please explain your answer.

CHAPTER 12: UNDERSTANDING THE INCARNATION OF JESUS CHRIST

1. How do we know that Jesus was really a man?

2. How do we know that Jesus was the Son of God?

3. What makes Jesus different than the prophets who founded other religions?

4. Why is it so important to believe that the "virgin birth" of Jesus is truth?

5. Why do you think it was so important to us for God the Son to become a human being?

- 95 -

Name: _____

Date: _____

CHAPTER 13: UNDERSTANDING THE NEW COVENANT

1. Why was there a need for a New Covenant?

2. There are many reasons why the New Covenant is a better and more powerful covenant. List the three (3) reasons you think are the most significant?

   -

   -

   -

3. How did Jesus mediate this New Covenant for us?

4. What price did Jesus pay to redeem mankind? Explain.

5. How has Jesus redeemed us from:

   a. Sin?

   b. Death?

   c. The power of the devil?

6. Why do you think it is important to enter into this New Covenant?

CHAPTER 14: UNDERSTANDING CHRIST'S RESURRECTION AND ASCENSION

1. How long was the body of Jesus in the grave?

2. Why did the soul and spirit of Christ descend into Sheol / Hades?

3. Using the Scripture references for Question 14.5, name three instances where Jesus appeared to people after His resurrection?

   -
   -
   -

4. How was Jesus' resurrected body different from his old body?

5. What is it so important that we believe in the resurrection of Jesus?

6. What does the "second coming of Jesus Christ" mean?

CHAPTER 15: UNDERSTANDING SIN AND INIQUITY

1. What is Original Sin?

2. What is Actual Sin?

3. Why do we need to know what sin is?

4. Give at least two (2) reasons why do we need to keep the Ten Commandments?

    •

    •

5. What is iniquity?

6. How does iniquity affect our lives?

7. How do we find deliverance from our iniquities?

CHAPTER 16: UNDERSTANDING THE FIRST COMMANDMENT

1. What does this commandment forbid us to do?

2. How do we keep this commandment?

3. Why is this commandment so important?

4. Restate this commandment in the positive. (For example, "You shall . . .)

CHAPTER 17: UNDERSTANDING THE SECOND COMMANDMENT

1. What does this commandment forbid us to do?

2. How do we keep this commandment?

3. Read Matt. 19:16-30.   Explain how the rich, young ruler broke this commandment?

4. Restate this commandment in the positive. "You shall . . ."

CHAPTER 18: UNDERSTANDING THE THIRD COMMANDMENT

1. Name four ways this commandment can be broken?

   -

   -

   -

   -

2. How do we keep this commandment?

3. Why do you think God is so concerned about how we use His name?

4. What is the difference between an oath and a vow? How are they similar?

5. How was the meaning of this commandment expanded in the New Testament?

CHAPTER 19: UNDERSTANDING THE FOURTH COMMANDMENT

1. Under the Old Covenant, how did the nation of Israel keep this commandment?

2. Under the New Covenant, how do we keep this commandment?

3. What is the significant difference in the meaning of this commandment from the Old Covenant to the New Covenant?

4. If the Sabbath is Saturday, why do most churches have services on Sunday?

5. Why is it important to attend church services regularly?

6. Restate this commandment in the negative. "You shall not . . ."

CHAPTER 20: UNDERSTANDING THE FIFTH COMMANDMENT

1. Give three (3) examples of how you would keep this commandment.

   •

   •

   •

2. Why would God want us to learn how to obey this commandment?

3. Besides your parents, name four (4) other types of authorities you should obey.

   •

   •

   •

   •

4. When are we NOT required to obey our parents or those in authority over us?

5. Restate this commandment in the negative. "You shall not . . ."

CHAPTER 21: UNDERSTANDING THE SIXTH COMMANDMENT

1. What does this commandment forbid us to do?

2. Name three (3) ways Jesus expanded the meaning of this commandment.

   •

   •

   •

3. When does being angry become sinful?

4. Why do you think Jesus expanded the meaning of this commandment?

5. Restate this commandment in the positive. "You shall . . ."

CHAPTER 22: UNDERSTANDING THE SEVENTH COMMANDMENT

1. What does this commandment forbid us to do?

2. How did Jesus expand the meaning of this commandment?

3. Why do you think Jesus expanded the meaning of this commandment?

4. In the New Testament we are warned to flee fornication. List at least four (4) meaning of fornication.

   -
   -
   -
   -

5. I Cor. 6:19 says that your body is the "temple of the Holy Spirit." What does this mean?

6. Restate this commandment in the positive. "You shall . . ."

CHAPTER 23: UNDERSTANDING THE EIGHTH COMMANDMENT

1. Give four (4) examples of how you could break this commandment.

   -
   -
   -
   -

2. Give three (3) examples of how you can keep this commandment.

   -
   -
   -

3. Why is stealing offensive to God?

4. Restate this commandment in the positive. "You shall . . ."

CHAPTER 24: UNDERSTANDING THE NINTH COMMANDMENT

1. What does this commandment forbid us to do?

2. Give at least three (3) examples of lying?

    •

    •

    •

3. Why is lying offensive to God?

4. Restate this commandment in the positive. "You shall . . ."

CHAPTER 25: UNDERSTANDING THE TENTH COMMANDMENT

1. What does it mean "to covet"?

2. Give at least three (3) examples of covetousness.

    •

    •

    •

3. What lesson does Jesus teach about coveting? (Luke 12:15)

4. How is covetousness linked to the sin of idolatry?

5. Restate this commandment in the positive. "You shall . . ."

CHAPTER 26: UNDERSTANDING SALVATION

1. Explain what it means to be "drawn" by God?

2. Once we accept Jesus Christ as our Savior, He desires that we become His disciple. What does every disciple of Christ need?

3. What are the six (6) Principles of the Doctrine of Christ that are to be our spiritual foundation? (Heb. 6:1-3)

   •

   •

   •

   •

   •

   •

4. Have you accepted Jesus Christ as your Savior? Explain.

5. Have you laid all six of the Principles of the Doctrine of Christ? Explain.

- 122 -

CHAPTER 27: UNDERSTANDING REPENTANCE FROM DEAD WORKS

1. Why are man-made religious observances or ceremonies "dead works"?

2. When do good works become "dead works"?

3. List at least three (3) examples of "dead works."

    •

    •

    •

4. What does it mean to "repent from dead works"?

5. How do we "repent from dead works"?

6. What would this principle be the first one that we must lay in our spiritual foundation?

7. Has the principle of "repentance from dead works" been laid as part of your spiritual foundation? Explain.

CHAPTER 28: UNDERSTANDING FAITH TOWARD GOD

1. Because there is nothing we can do to earn our salvation or to save ourselves, the second principle is to turn our "faith toward God" to justify us.

   What does it mean to be justified?

2. Why is it necessary to be justified?

3. How are sinners justified by a holy God?

   -
   -
   -

4. How do we know if we are justified?

5. Have you turned your faith toward God to justify you by accepting Jesus as your Savior? Explain.

CHAPTER 29: UNDERSTANDING WATER BAPTISM

1. What are the three (3) baptisms that make up the Doctrine of Baptisms?

    •

    •

    •

2. How do we become "partakers" of Christ's death and burial that joins us to Christ?

3. What spiritual change occurs in us when we are water baptized?

4. What does the "circumcision of heart" mean? Why is it necessary?

    •

    •

5. What does it mean to be "born again"?

6. Why do we need to be "born again"? Explain.

CHAPTER 29: UNDERSTANDING WATER BAPTISM (cont.)

7. Who should be water baptized?

8. Why must our water baptism need to be more than a sign that we are believers in the Lord Jesus Christ?

9. When does the experience of water baptism become a rite rather than a life changing sacrament?

10. Do you need to be water baptized? Why or why not?

CHAPTER 30: UNDERSTANDING THE HOLY SPIRIT

1. Define the Holy Spirit.

2. Explain how the Holy Spirit works in the lives of sinners.

3. Explain how the Holy Spirit worked in the life of Jesus.

4. What is the "unpardonable sin"?

5. How should we regard the Holy Spirit?

Name: _____

Date: _____

CHAPTER 31: UNDERSTANDING THE BAPTISM OF THE HOLY SPIRIT

1. What do we need the Baptism of the Holy Spirit? List at least six (6) reasons.

   •

   •

   •

   •

   •

   •

2. How are Water Baptism and the Baptism of the Holy Spirit connected?

3. How do we receive the Baptism of the Holy Spirit?

4. What is the "speaking in tongues"?

5. Why is "speaking in tongues" necessary?

CHAPTER 32: UNDERSTANDING THE BAPTISM OF FIRE

1. Define the Baptism of Fire.

2. Define Sanctification.

3. Why do we need to be "sanctified"?

4. What is the difference between chastening and punishment?

5. List three (3) examples of what could be regarded as a Baptism of Fire.

   -

   -

   -

6. What "Baptism of Fire" have you experienced? How were you perfected or strengthened through this experience? How were you changed?

CHAPTER 33: UNDERSTANDING THE LAYING ON OF HANDS

1. Give an example of the Laying on of Hands in the Old Testament.

2. Give an example of the Laying on of Hands in the New Testament.

3. Read Acts 9 and Acts 19. Name someone in the Bible who received the Gift of the Holy Spirit by the Laying on of Hands.

4. What is the purpose of the Laying on of Hands:

   - For Confirmation?

   - For Ordination?

   - With Prophecy?

5. Have you ever been ministered to by the Laying on of Hands? Explain.

CHAPTER 34: UNDERSTANDING THE RESURRECTION OF THE DEAD

1. What happens to your body, soul and spirit when you die?

2. Describe Paradise.

3. What is the difference between Sheol/Hades and Hell?

4. Will you recognize people after you die? Explain.

5. Answer the following questions about the "First Resurrection":

   - Who will be resurrected?

   - What will happen to them?

   - Describe the new body they will receive.

CHAPTER 34: UNDERSTANDING THE RESURRECTION OF THE DEAD
(cont.)

6. Answer the following questions about the "Second Resurrection":

- Who will be resurrected?

- What will happen to them?

7. Have you experienced the resurrection power of God in your life? Explain.

8. Why is the Doctrine of Resurrection so important to our spiritual foundation?

CHAPTER 35: UNDERSTANDING ETERNAL JUDGMENT

1. Who will be judged at the first judgment – the Judgment Seat of Christ?

2. When will this first judgment take place?

3. Who will be judged at the second judgment – the Great White Throne Judgment?

4. List at least four (4) areas in our lives that God will judge?

5. What is the purpose of these judgments?

6. How do we experience God's judgment in this lifetime?

CHAPTER 36: UNDERSTANDING THE APOSTLE'S CREED

1. Define the term "creed".

2. Why should we memorize the Apostles' Creed?

CHAPTER 37: UNDERSTANDING CHRIST'S CHURCH

1. What does the term "church" mean?

2. Give at least three (3) mysteries concerning Christ and His Church.

   •

   •

   •

   •

3. What is our responsibility as a member of Christ's Church?

4. Are you a member of Christ's Church? Explain.

- 142 -

CHAPTER 38: UNDERSTANDING THE LOCAL CHURCH

1. What is the difference between the "Universal Church" and the "Local Church"?

2. What is the purpose of the Local Church?

3. How does the Local Church help us mature in Christ?

4. What are the blessings of being part of a Local Church?

5. What are the challenges of being part of a Local Church?

6. Are you a member of a Local Church? Explain.

- 143 -

CHAPTER 39: UNDERSTANDING WORSHIP

1. Why do you think worship involves sacrifice?

2. Worship in the Old Covenant differs from the worship in the New Covenant. Cite the differences in the chart below:

Question	Old Covenant	New Covenant
Who can worship?		
Who can enter God's presence?		
What happens to sin?		
Type of sacrifice required?		
Where can you worship?		

3. How do we worship God with our:

- Bodies?

- Service?

- Lips?

4. Why is it so important to praise God?

5. What song or hymn is your favorite? Explain.

CHAPTER 40: UNDERSTANDING PRAYER AND FASTING

1. Define prayer.

2. What is necessary for an effective prayer life? Name eighth (8) factors.

   •

   •

   •

   •

   •

   •

   •

   •

3. What is the benefit of being able to pray in tongues (in a spirit language)?

4. What hinders God from answering our prayers?

5. Why should we pray together?

6. Name at least five (5) things we should pray for in community or congregational prayer.

   -
   -
   -
   -
   -

7. Why is intercessory prayer important for the church?

8. Name three (3) types of fasts.

   -
   -
   -

9. Why is the purpose for fasting?

Name: _____

Date: _____

CHAPTER 41: UNDERSTANDING THE GIFTS OF THE HOLY SPIRIT

1. Define each of the following *gifts* of the Holy Spirit.

- Gift of Faith

- Gift of Miracles

- Gift of Healing

- Gift of Prophecy

- Gift of Tongues

- Gift of Interpretation of Tongues

- Gift of Wisdom

- Gift of Knowledge

- Gift of Discerning of spirits

2. How are these spiritual gifts of the Holy Spirit connected to our natural gifts?

3. What will happen if we do not develop and use our natural and spiritual gifts?

CHAPTER 42: UNDERSTANDING THE MINISTRIES OF THE HOLY SPIRIT

1. What is the difference between a calling and a ministry?

2. Define the following ministries. What is a(n) . . .

   - Apostle

   - Prophet

   - Evangelist

   - Pastor

   - Teacher

   - Governments

   - Helps

3. God often uses our natural gifts as a springboard for a spiritual ministry in the church. What do you feel your natural gift(s) is(are)?

4. Do you currently have a place of ministry in your church? Explain.

CHAPTER 43: UNDERSTANDING THE SACRAMENTS OF THE CHURCH

1. What are the two parts of a sacrament that distinguish it from a rite or ceremony?

2. Name the seven (7) sacraments.

-
-
-
-
-
-
-

3. Why do we need to experience these sacraments?

4. What should you do before participating in any sacrament?

CHAPTER 44: UNDERSTANDING THE LORD'S SUPPER

1. Compare the Lord's Supper of the New Covenant to the Passover of the Old Covenant.

	Passover	Lord's Supper
What is the sacrifice?		
What do the participants receive?		
What is remembered?		
What is celebrated?		

2. What is the outward sign or experience of this sacrament?

3. What is the inner spiritual work of this sacrament?

4. The Bible states that we are to examine ourselves before we take the Lord's Supper. What does it mean to examine yourself?

5. Why is it so important that we examine ourselves before we take the Lord's Supper?

- 156 -

CHAPTER 45: UNDERSTANDING FOOTWASHING

1. Why did Jesus institute the Sacrament of Footwashing?

2. What problem did the disciples have that we also have?

3. What is the outward sign or experience of this sacrament?

4. What is the inner spiritual work of this sacrament? (What happens to you when you wash someone's feet and they wash your feet?)

5. How often should you participate in the Sacrament of Footwashing?

6. Have you ever participated in a Sacrament of Footwashing? Explain.

CHAPTER 46: UNDERSTANDING DIVINE HEALING AND ANOINTING WITH OIL

1. How did sickness become part of the human experience?

2. How can we receive divine healing? Name seven (7) ways healing can be administered.

   •

   •

   •

   •

   •

   •

   •

3. What is an absolute necessity in order to receive divine healing?

4. What can prevent us from receiving healing?

5. What is more important – physical or spiritual healing? Explain.

CHAPTER 46:   UNDERSTANDING DIVINE HEALING AND ANOINTING
WITH OIL (cont.)

6. What is the outward experience of the Sacrament of Anointing with Oil?

7.   Why is oil used is this sacrament?

8. What is the important inner spiritual work of this sacrament?

9. What areas of our life need to be examined before we receive this sacrament?

CHAPTER 47: UNDERSTANDING THE SACRAMENT OF CONFIRMATION

1. What is the outward sign or experience of this sacrament?

2. What is the inner spiritual work of this sacrament?

3. Who administers this sacrament?

4. How do we prepare ourselves for this sacrament?

5. Why is this sacrament a necessity for believers?

CHAPTER 48: UNDERSTANDING MATRIMONY

1. What is the outward experience of the Sacrament of Matrimony?

2. What is the inner spiritual work of this sacrament?

3. Give at least three (3) reasons why God established the institution of marriage.

   •

   •

   •

4. Why would the Scriptures state the believers should not marry unbelievers?

5. What does it mean when the Scriptures state that wives are to submit to their husbands?

6. When does God permit divorce?

CHAPTER 49:   UNDERSTANDING THE PRESENTATION OF A CHILD TO GOD

1. What is the outward experience of this sacrament?

2. What is the spiritual work of this sacrament?

3. Does the parents' spiritual responsibility for their child end with the administration of this sacrament? Explain what God expects of parents.

4. What does God expect of children?

5. How are parents to discipline their children?

6. What are the characteristics of a Christian home?

CHAPTER 50: UNDERSTANDING GIVING

1. Why is it important to God that we become cheerful and generous givers?

2. What are eight (8) truths Jesus taught about giving?

   •

   •

   •

   •

   •

   •

   •

   •

3. What is a tithe?

4. Why are we to give a tithe of what we earn to our Local Church?

5. How do offerings and alms differ from a tithe?

6. Which aspect of giving do you think is the most difficult for people to accept? Explain.

CHAPTER 51: UNDERSTANDING THE CHRISTIAN LIFESTYLE

1. Describe the Christian lifestyle. How does it differ from the lifestyle of the world?

2. What Christ-like qualities should others be able to see in us?

3. What procedure should be followed if there is a disagreement or dispute between two Christians? (Reference Matt. 18:17)

    Step 1:

    Step 2:

    Step 3:

    Step 4:

4. As a member of a Local Church, what is our responsibility if we are aware of a member who is practicing sin?

5. Why should we be committed to living a Christian lifestyle?